**Mensa** KiDS

TRAIN your BRAIN

PUZZLE BOOK

LEVEL 3
FOR ADVANCED PUZZLERS

THIS IS A CARLTON BOOK

Text and puzzle content copyright © British Mensa
Limited 1994 & 1997 & 2010
Design and artwork copyright © Carlton Books Limited
1994 & 1997 & 2010 & 2014

This edition published in 2014 by Carlton Books Limited
An imprint of the Carlton Publishing Group
20 Mortimer Street, London, W1T 3JW

10 9 8 7 6 5 4 3 2 1

A catalogue record for this book is available from the British Library.

ISBN 978-1-78312-075-8

Printed in Dongguan, China

Senior Editor: Alexandra Koken
Designed by: Katie Baxendale
Production: Marion Storz

Mensa KIDS

TRAIN
your
BRAIN

PUZZLE BOOK

LEVEL 3
FOR ADVANCED PUZZLERS

CARLTON
KiDS

INTRODUCTION

RECKON YOU'RE A GENIUS?

You just might be if you can crack the fiendish teasers in this little book.

This **LEVEL 3** puzzle book is packed with questions to test your verbal and numerical reasoning. To solve them you'll need the ability to think logically, plus some staying power when the problems get tough.

Now, put on your thinking cap, turn the page and let the training begin!

LEVEL 3 is the third in the Train Your Brain Puzzle Book series: check out **LEVEL 1** for beginners' puzzles, and **LEVEL 2** for intermediate teasers.

WHAT IS MENSA?

Mensa is the international society for people with a high IQ. We have more than 100,000 members in over 40 countries worldwide. The society's aims are:

* to identify and foster human intelligence for the benefit of humanity
* to encourage research in the nature, characteristics, and uses of intelligence
* to provide a stimulating intellectual and social environment for its members

Anyone with an IQ score in the top two per cent of the population is eligible to become a member of Mensa — are you the "one in 50" we've been looking for? Mensa membership offers an excellent range of benefits:

* Networking and social activities nationally and around the world
* Special Interest Groups — hundreds of chances to pursue your hobbies and interests — from art to zoology!
* Monthly members' magazine and regional newsletters
* Local meetings — from games challenges to food and drink
* National and international weekend gatherings and conferences
* Intellectually stimulating lectures and seminars
* Access to the worldwide SIGHT network for travellers and hosts

For more information about Mensa:
www.mensa.org.uk
Telephone: +44 (0) 1902 772771
E-mail: enquiries@mensa.org.uk
British Mensa Ltd., St John's House, St John's Square, Wolverhampton, WV2 4AH

PUZZLE 1

Move up or across from the bottom left-hand 8 to the top right-hand 7. Collect nine numbers and add them together. What is the lowest you can score?

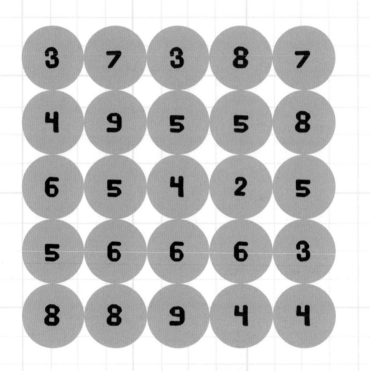

THE HARD ONES ARE FUN!

1	2	3
11	7	5
13	17	?

PUZZLE 2

Find a number to complete
the square.

Hint: Is this
prime time?

A   B   C

PUZZLE 3

Which of the three faces completes
the series? Is it A, B or C?

PUZZLE 4

Start at any corner and follow the lines.
Add up the first four numbers you meet
and then add on the corner number. How
many different routes will add up to 21?

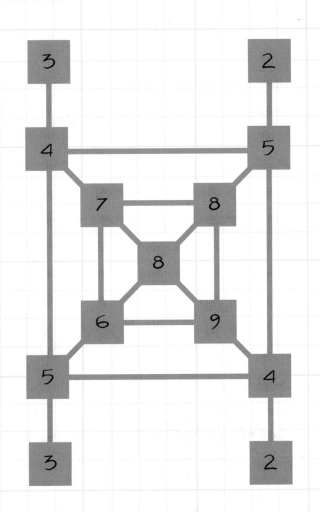

PUZZLE 5

Which of the figures above is the odd one out?

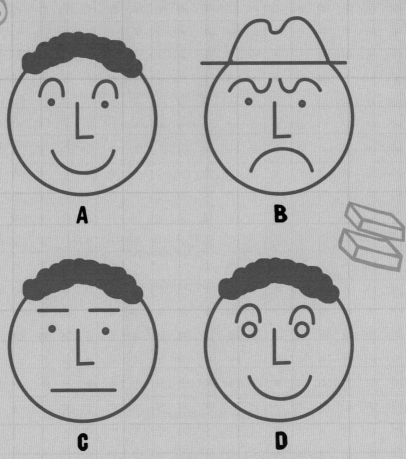

A   B

C   D

PUZZLE 6

Which of the faces is the odd one out?

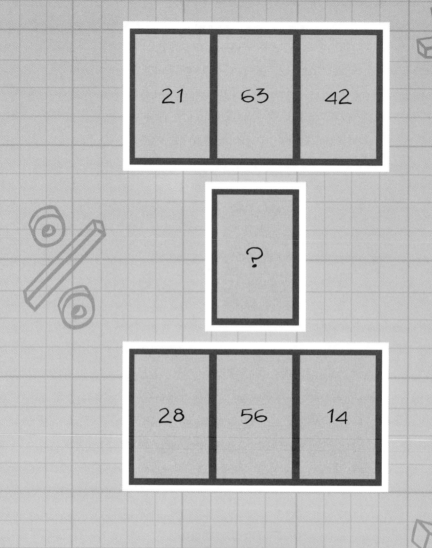

PUZZLE 7

Place in the middle box a number larger than 1. If the number is the correct one, all the other numbers can be divided by it without leaving any remainder. What is the number?

PUZZLE 8

What number should replace the
question mark?

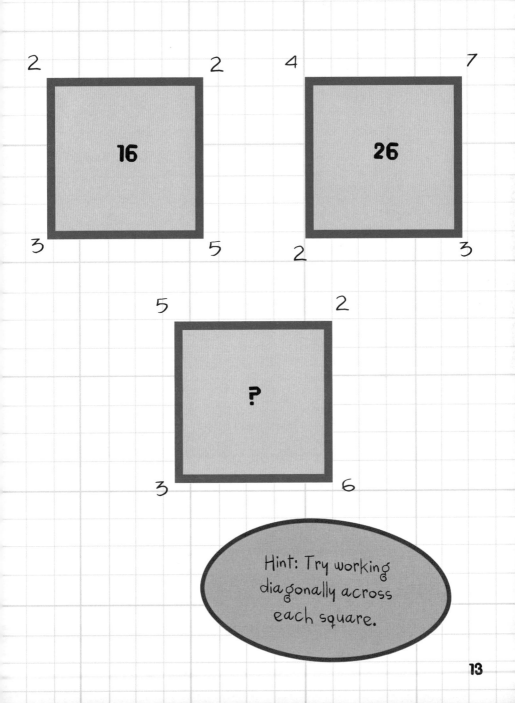

2   2   4   7

16   26

3   5   2   3

5   2

?

3   6

Hint: Try working
diagonally across
each square.

KEEP FOCUSED!

PUZZLE 9

What number completes the final figure?

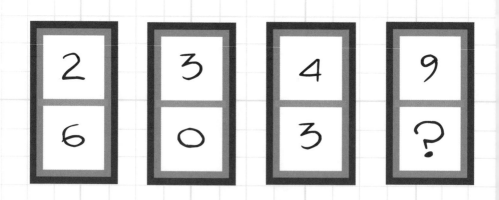

Hint: The answer is totally in line!

PUZZLE 10

Each sector of the circle follows a pattern.
What number should replace
the question mark?

4	54	5
3	63	6
7	27	2
9	19	1
8	?	2

PUZZLE 11

What number replaces the question mark?

PUZZLE 12

Which block completes the square?

4	8	3	2	6
8	5	3	7	9
3	3	2	4	8
2		4	9	3
6		8	3	7

A
5
3

B
7
9

C
4
2

PUZZLE 13

Here is an unusual safe. Each of the buttons must be pressed only once in the correct order to open it. The last button is marked F. The number of moves and the direction are marked on each button. Thus 1i would mean one move in, whilst 1o would mean one move out. 1c would mean one move clockwise and 1a would mean one move anti-clockwise. Which button is the first you must press? Here's a clue: look on the inner circle.

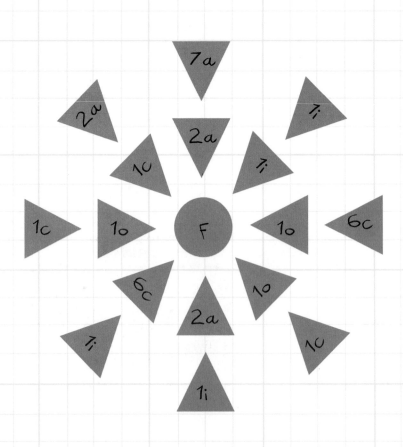

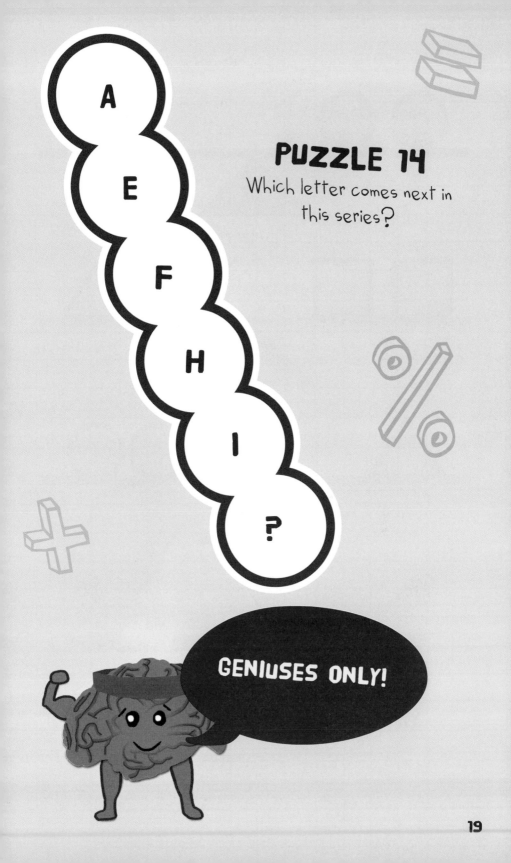

PUZZLE 14

Which letter comes next in this series?

A E F H I ?

GENIUSES ONLY!

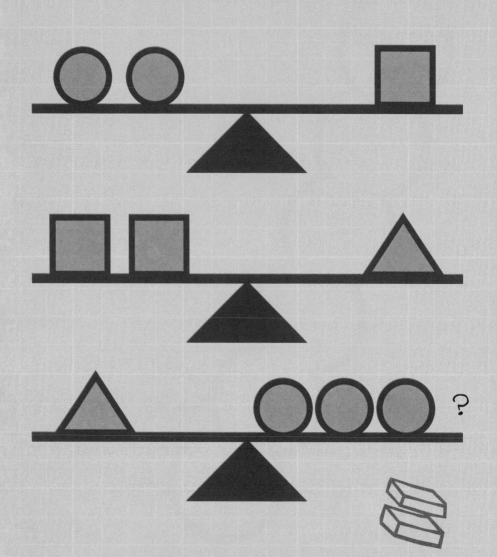

PUZZLE 15

Each of these pairs of scales is perfectly balanced. Use logic to discover which symbol is needed to balance the third pair. Is it a square, circle or triangle?

PUZZLE 16

Each slice of this cake adds up to the same number. Also each ring of the cake totals the same. What number should appear in the blanks?

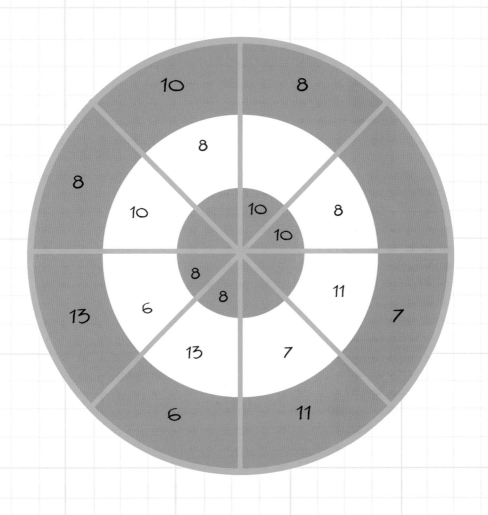

PUZZLE 17

These figures form a logical series.
Which is the odd one out?

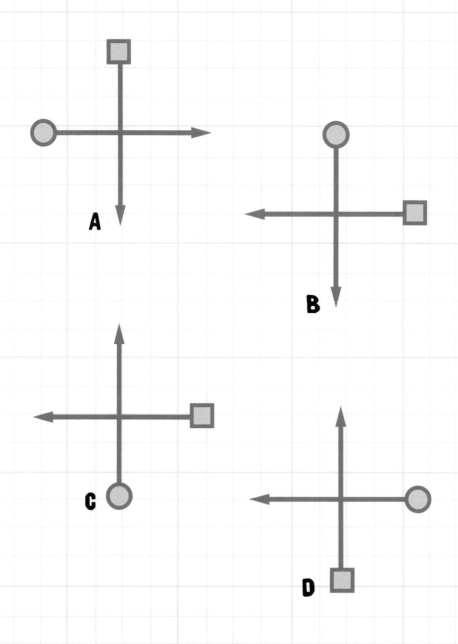

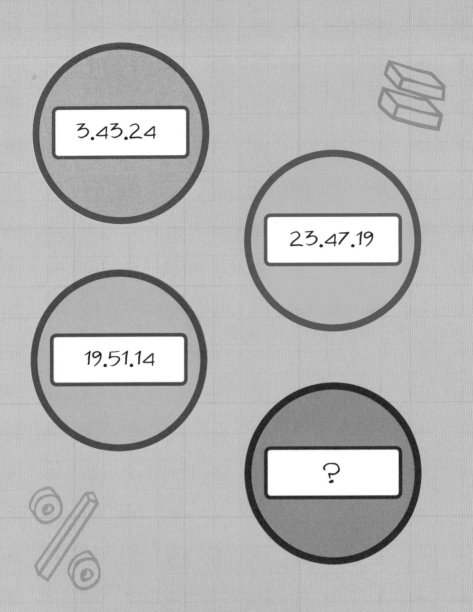

3.43.24

23.47.19

19.51.14

?

PUZZLE 18

The times on these digital watches form a series. What time should be shown on the final watch?

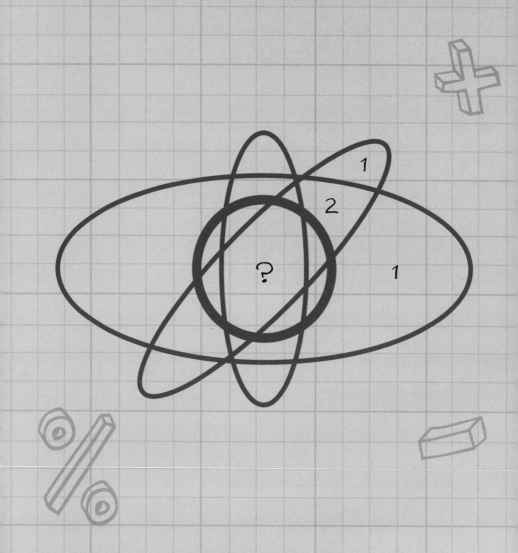

PUZZLE 19

If you look carefully you should see why the numbers are written as they are. What number should replace the question mark?

PUZZLE 20

These figures form a logical series.
Which is the odd one out?

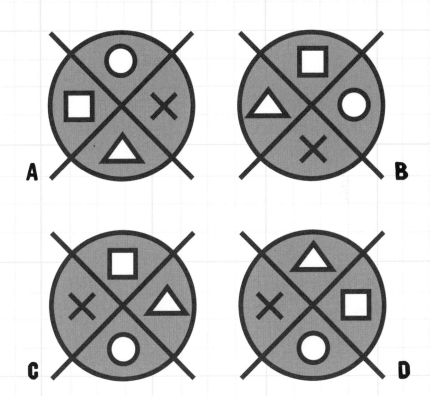

A

B

C

D

YOU'RE ONE
SMART COOKIE!

PUZZLE 21

Which matchstick man is needed to
continue the series below?

PUZZLE 22

Copy the cake slices out carefully and rearrange them to find the birthday. How old were the twins?

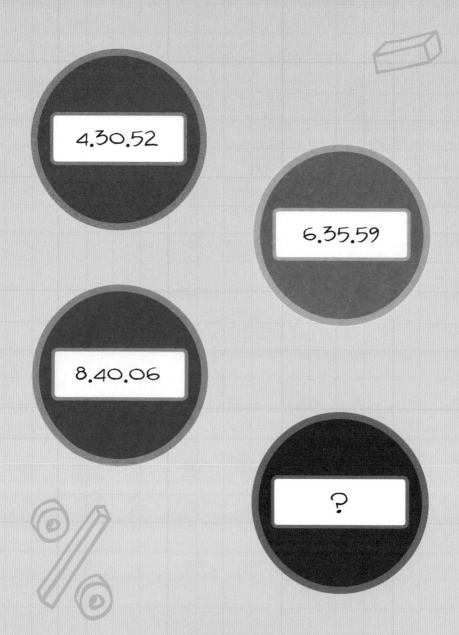

4.30.52

6.35.59

8.40.06

?

PUZZLE 23

There is a logical connection between the times shown on these digital watches. What time should appear on the fourth watch?

PUZZLE 24

Which of the figures below is the odd one out?

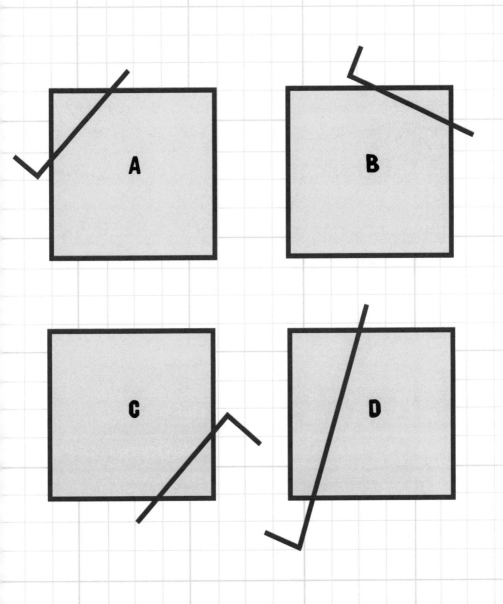

PUZZLE 25

Start at the A and move to B passing through various parts of the cow. There is a number in each part and these must be added together. What is the lowest total you can find?

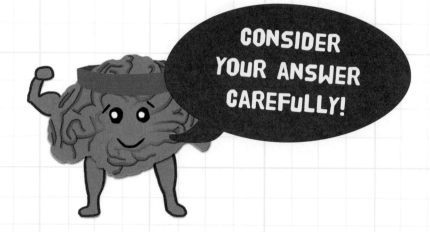

CONSIDER YOUR ANSWER CAREFULLY!

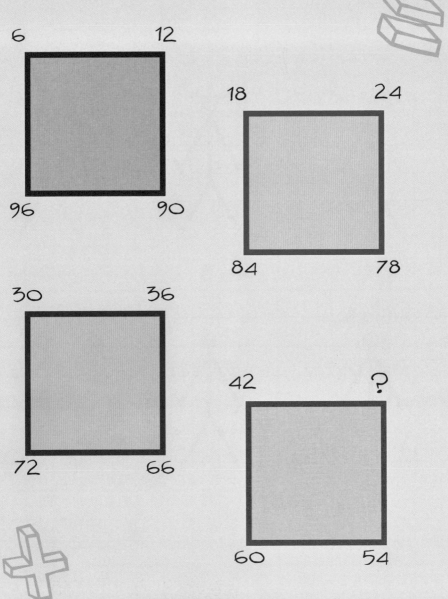

6 12
96 90

18 24
84 78

30 36
72 66

42 ?
60 54

PUZZLE 26

The numbers surrounding these squares are all connected. Try to find one which will replace the question mark.

PUZZLE 27

Can you spot the odd
figure out?

PUZZLE 28

Each sector of this wheel has a number written on it. Using the numbers shown how many different ways are there to add four numbers together to make a total of 14? A number can be used more than once, but a group cannot be repeated in a different order.

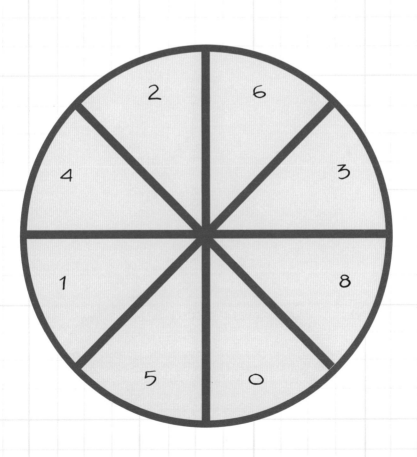

PUZZLE 29

What number will replace the question mark in the bottom triangle?
This is a real toughie.

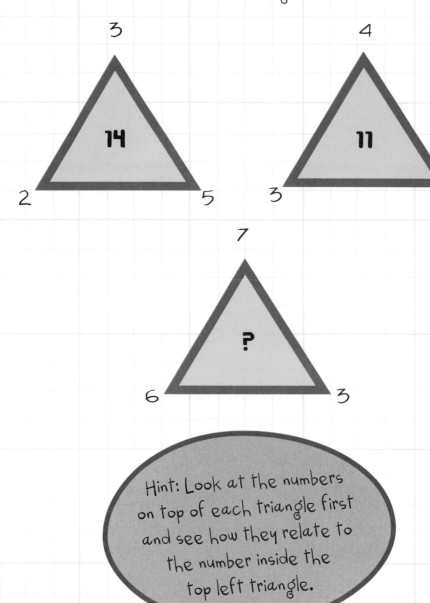

3

14

2   5

4

11

3   6

7

?

6   3

Hint: Look at the numbers on top of each triangle first and see how they relate to the number inside the top left triangle.

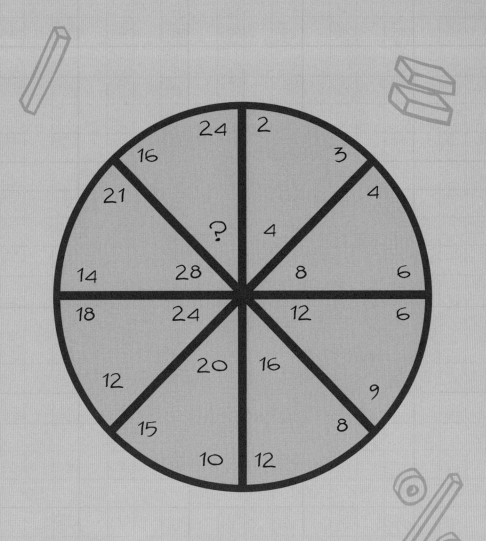

PUZZLE 30

Find a number to replace the question mark. This is a hard one so here is a big hint: Take a look at your 2, 3, and 4 times tables.

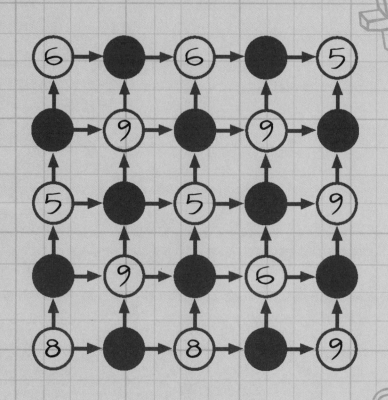

PUZZLE 31

Move from the bottom left-hand 8 to the top right-hand 5 adding together all five numbers. Each blank circle is worth minus 4 and this should be taken away from your total each time you meet one. What is the lowest total and how many different routes are there to find it?

A E C G E I ?

PUZZLE 32
Find the next letter in the series.

THINK HARD!

37

PUZZLE 33

Since 100 AD has a new century e.g. 200, 1000, 1900 and so on, ever started on a Sunday?

8	1	3	4
6	2	3	1
9	4	2	3
5	1	3	?

A   **B**   **C**   **D**

PUZZLE 34

The numbers in column D are linked in some way to those in A, B and C. What number replaces the question mark?

A   B   C   D

PUZZLE 35

Which is the odd one out in this
series? Is it A, B, C or D?

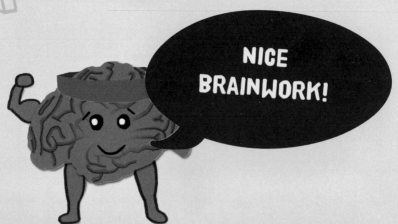

NICE BRAINWORK!

PUZZLE 36

The boxes represent the gas, water and electricity services. You have to connect each service by a line drawn to each house. The lines must never cross each other, nor must they cross one of the boxes or one of the houses. How many ways of doing this are there — three ways, two ways, or one way? Or is it impossible?

GAS   WATER   ELECTRICITY

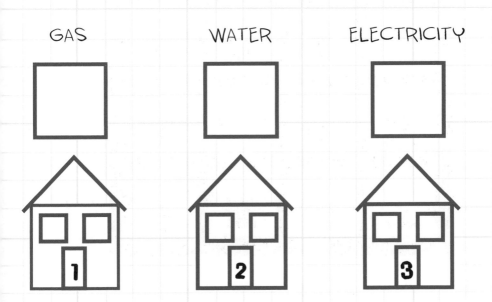

PUZZLE 37

Each symbol is worth a number. The total of the symbols can be found alongside each row and column. What number should replace the question mark?

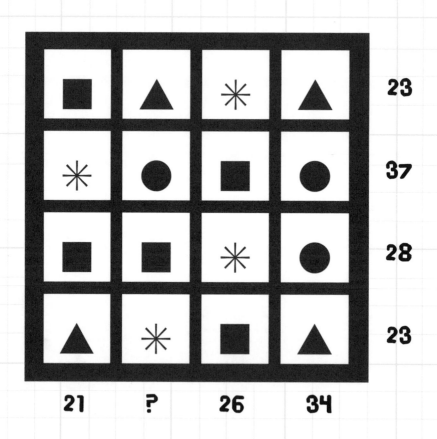

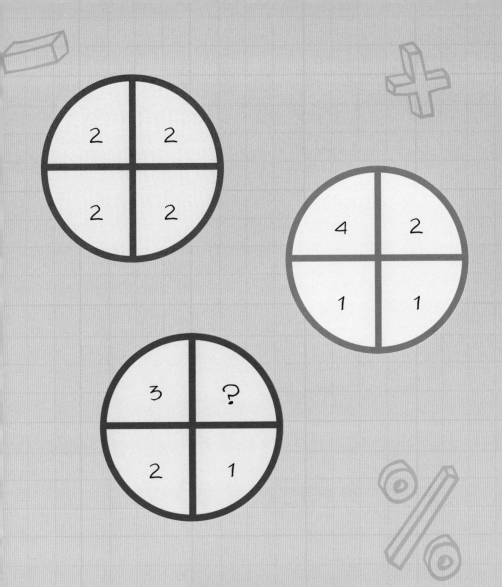

PUZZLE 38

Each circle works according to the same strange logic. When you have cracked it you should be able to complete the final circle with a number.

PUZZLE 39

Scrooge was no fool. He saved the ends of candles, melted them down and made new candles out of them. If 4 ends would make a new candle, how many candles would he get in total when he had burned 48 new ones? Beware! This is not as easy as it looks. Your first answer is partly correct, but you must think one stage further.

PUZZLE 40

On the planet Venox the coins used are 1V, 2V, 5V, 10V, 20V and 50V. A Venoxian has 2,349V in his squiggly bank. He has the same number of five kinds of coin. How many of each are there and what are they?

DON'T GIVE UP!

PUZZLE 41

Find the odd number out in the circle below.

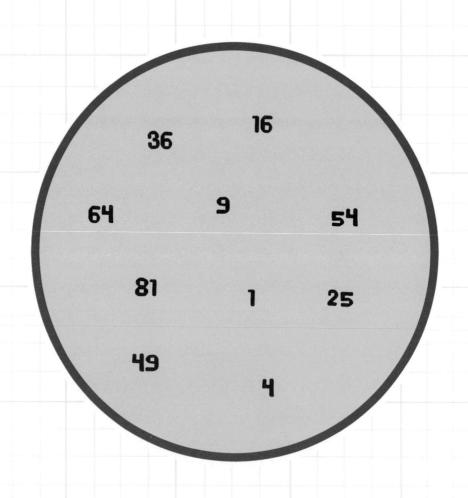

PUZZLE 42

A bottle factory melts down broken old bottles to make new ones. If they start with the remains of 279 bottles, and they can get one new one out of three old ones, how many new bottles can be made in total? Beware! Even the new ones get broken, and you have to think this one right through to the very end.

PUZZLE 43

Replace each question mark with plus, minus, multiply or divide. Each sign can be used more than once. When the correct ones have been used the sum will be completed. What are the signs?

| 4 | ? | 5 | ? | 3 | ? | 8 | | = | 24 |

PUZZLE 44

What number should replace the question mark to continue the series?

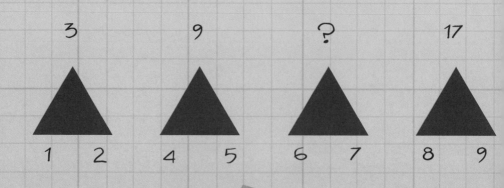

3 9 ? 17

1 2   4 5   6 7   8 9

| 2 | 4 | 7 | 14 | 17 | 34 | 37 | ? |

PUZZLE 45

What is the next number in this series?

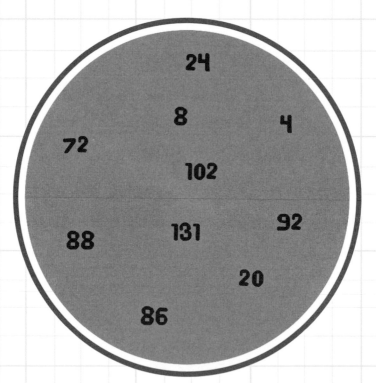

PUZZLE 46

Find the odd number out. Is it 102, 131 or 72?

PUZZLE 47

What is the lowest number of lines needed to divide the bear so that you can find the numbers 1, 2, 3, 4, 5 and 6 in each section?

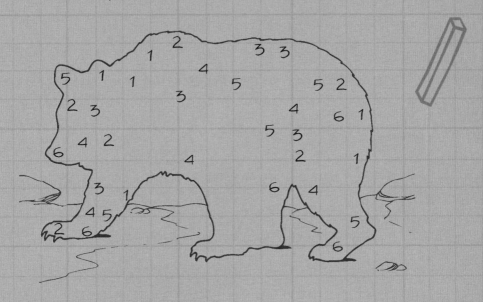

PUZZLE 48

Follow the arrows and find the longest possible route. How many boxes have been entered?

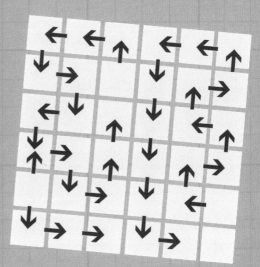

PUZZLE 49

Scrooge has a thrifty habit of saving soap. From the remains of three bars he can make one new one. How many bars can he make, in total, from the remains of nine new ones?

| 2 | 7 | 8 | 13 | 14 | 19 | 20 | 25 | ? |

PUZZLE 50
What number would continue the series?

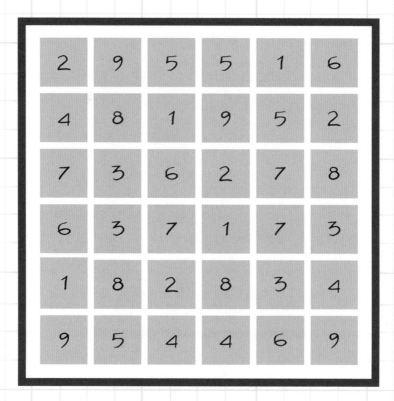

2	9	5	5	1	6
4	8	1	9	5	2
7	3	6	2	7	8
6	3	7	1	7	3
1	8	2	8	3	4
9	5	4	4	6	9

PUZZLE 51

Divide up the box into six identical shapes. The numbers in each shape add up to the same. How is this done?

A REAL BRAIN-TWISTER!

PUZZLE 52

What number continues the series?

| 1 | 4 | 8 | 11 | 15 | 18 | 22 | ? |

PUZZLE 53
Which number is the odd one out?

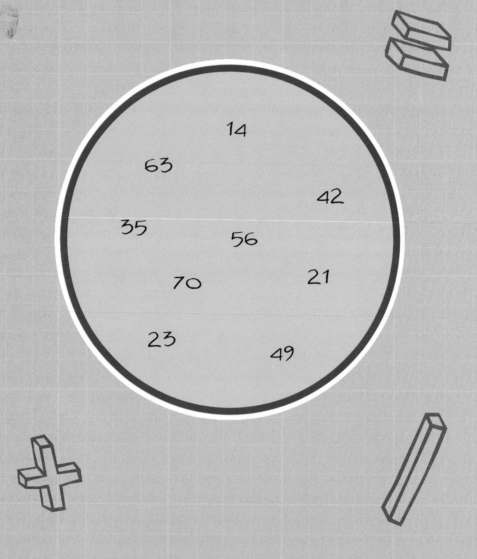

14

63

42

35

56

70

21

23

49

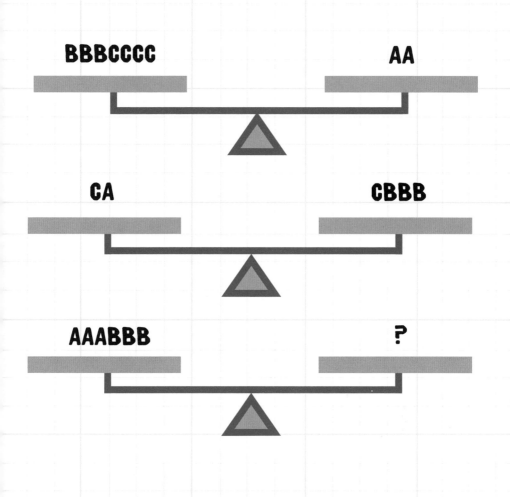

PUZZLE 54

Scales 1 and 2 are in perfect balance.
How many Cs are needed to
balance the third set?

PUZZLE 55

Old Scrooge recycles blunt and used wax crayons. From 10 old crayons he can make a brand new one. How many can he produce in total if he starts off with 200 crayons? Be warned, you must follow the logic right through to the end.

PUZZLE 56

How many squares of any size can you see in the grid?

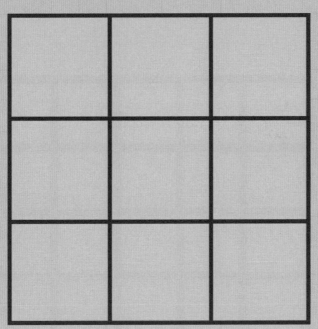

YOU'LL GET THE ANSWER!

PUZZLE 57

How many squares of any size can you find in this diagram?

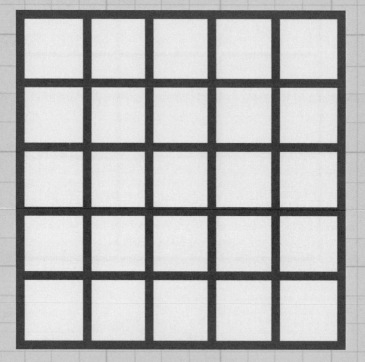

A   D

J   G

A   E

M   I

A   F

?   K

PUZZLE 58

Which letter should replace the question mark?

Hint: In each square the letters progress through the alphabet missing a number of letters at each step.

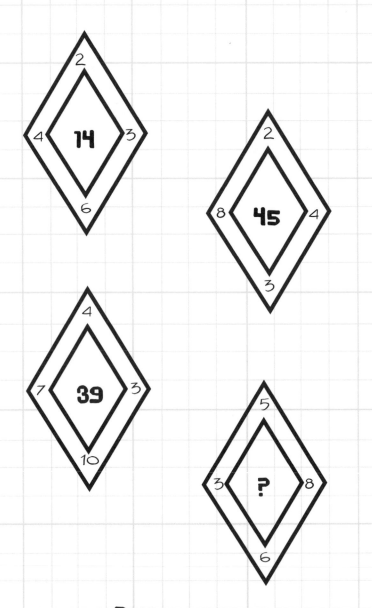

PUZZLE 59

The numbers in these diamonds obey a formula that involves adding, multiplying and subtracting the four outer numbers (in the same order around each diamond). Work out which number should go in the final diamond.

PUZZLE 60

Which squares contain the
same numbers?

	A	B	C	D	E
1	4 7 4 8	2 2 1	1 3 8 9	1 5 9 3	7 7 1 8
2	3 1 2	8 8 8 8	4 3 2 1	3 3 4 4	2 3 9 1
3	8 2 1 4	5 6 8 7	3 9 4 5	9 9 9 9	6 7 8 7
4	5 6 6 5	2 3 3 3	7 1 8 7	5 5 6 1	1 5 2 3
5	1 7 7 8	9 8 2 1	6 7 6 7	6 4 1 5	4 4 2 2

PUZZLE 61

Find a number to replace the
question mark.

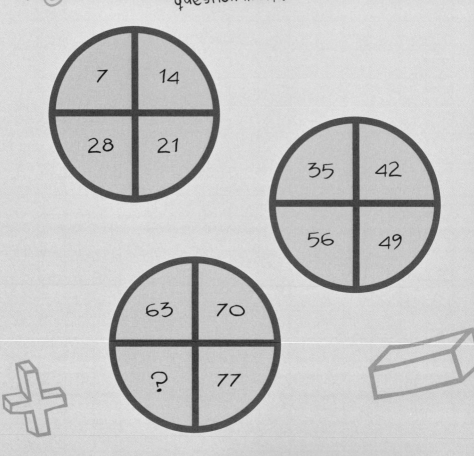

First circle:
- 7, 14
- 28, 21

Second circle:
- 35, 42
- 56, 49

Third circle:
- 63, 70
- ?, 77

WHAT A CHALLENGE!

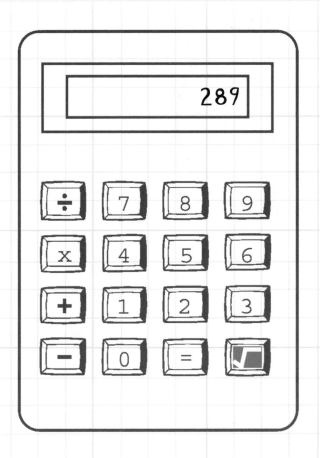

PUZZLE 62

What is the least number of buttons you must press to turn the number shown on the calculator into 17?

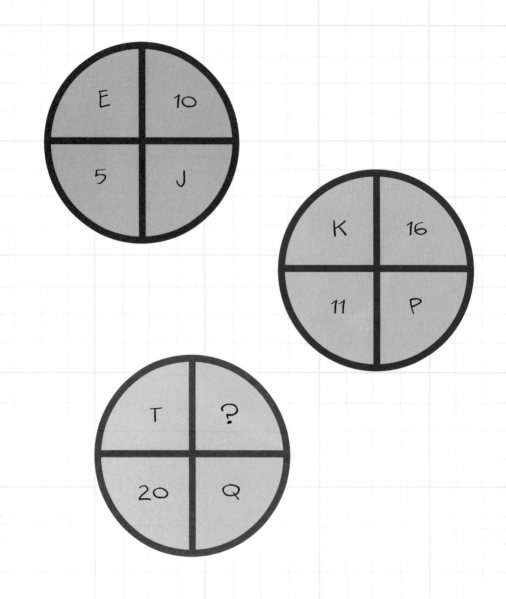

PUZZLE 63

Can you replace the question mark
with the missing number?

PUZZLE 64

Which cube is the odd one out?

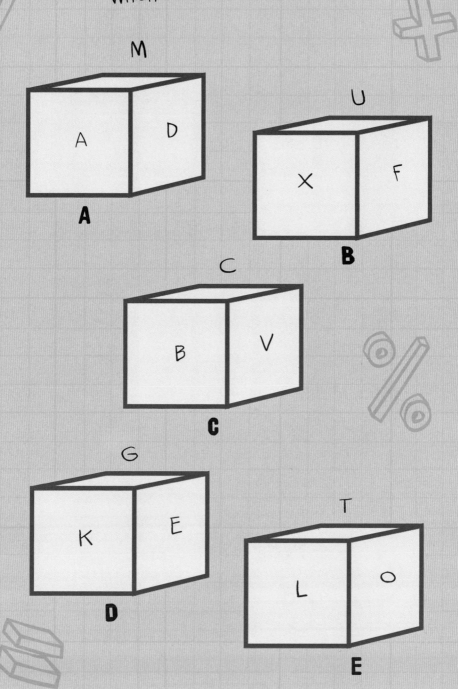

M

A   D

A

U

X   F

B

C

B   V

C

G

K   E

D

T

L   O

E

PUZZLE 65

Fill in the empty boxes, using two numbers only, so that every line adds up to 25. What number should replace the question mark?

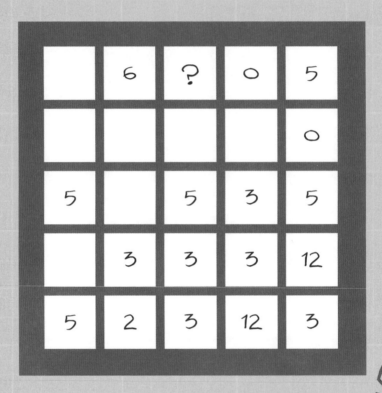

	6	?	0	5
				0
5		5	3	5
	3	3	3	12
5	2	3	12	3

CHALLENGE YOUR FRIENDS!

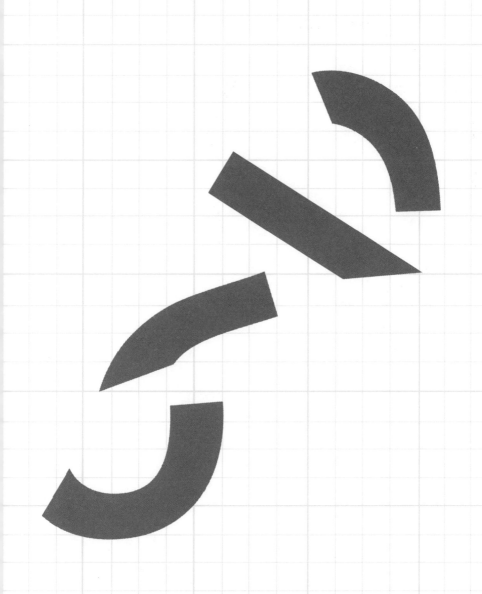

PUZZLE 66

Copy out these shapes carefully and
rearrange them to form a number.
What is it?

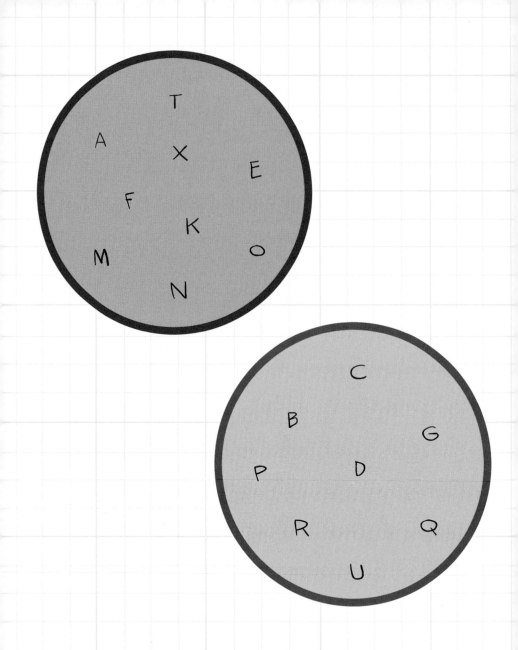

PUZZLE 67

Which letter would you move from the circle on the left to that on the right?

PUZZLE 68

To zap the spaceship find the number which, when multiplied by itself, will equal the total of the numbers shown. What is the number?

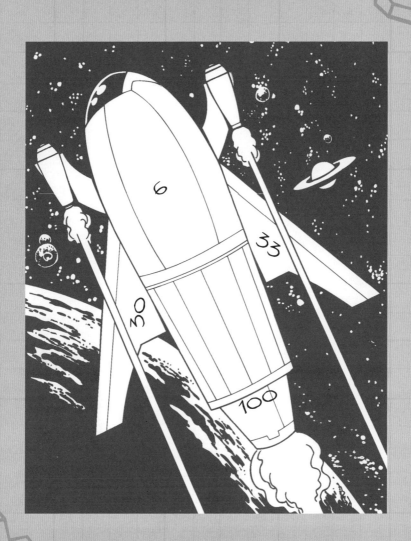

PUZZLE 69

Which letter would logically replace the question mark in this mathematical box? Remember that there is an easy way to convert letters to numbers. Is the answer P, F or R?

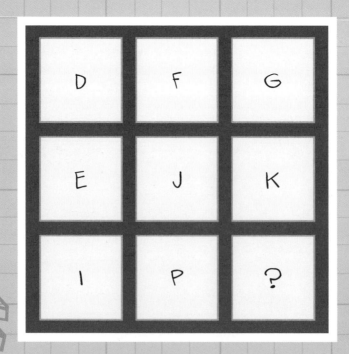

Number 9

1:35

Number 11

1:28

Number 13

1:37

Number 4

2:02

Number 8

1:07

PUZZLE 70

The time these cars take to complete one lap (given in minutes and seconds) is in some strange way linked to the car's number. Which car is the odd one out?

PUZZLE 71

How many 2s can be found in this Triceratops?

Find a letter to replace the question mark in this mathematical box. Remember that letters may easily be changed into numbers.

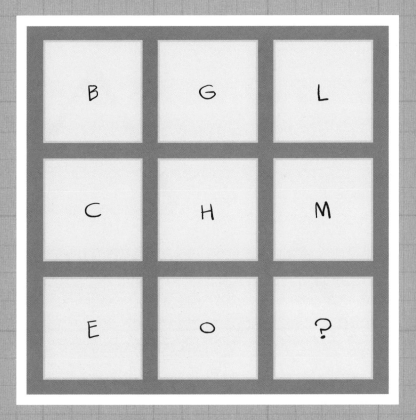

Find a number to complete the final triangle.

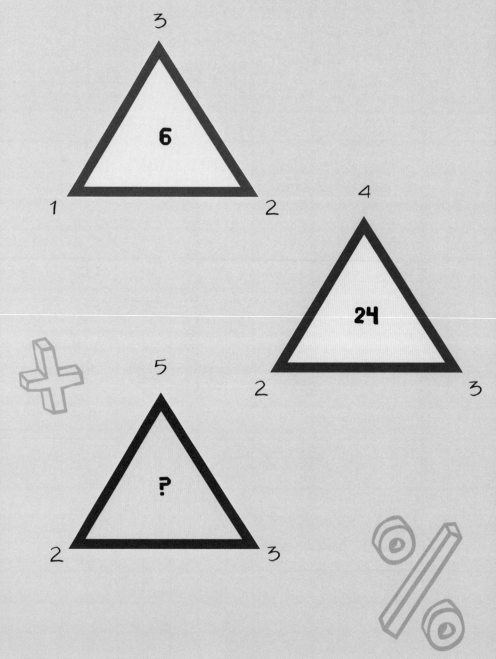

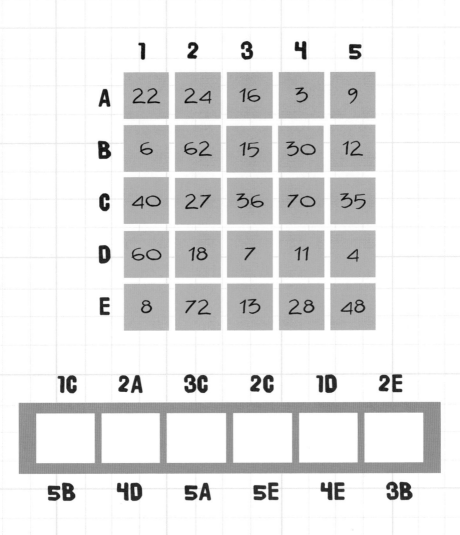

	1	2	3	4	5
A	22	24	16	3	9
B	6	62	15	30	12
C	40	27	36	70	35
D	60	18	7	11	4
E	8	72	13	28	48

1C 2A 3C 2C 1D 2E

5B 4D 5A 5E 4E 3B

PUZZLE 74

Find the correct six numbers to put in the frame. There are two choices for each square, for example 1A would give the number 22. When the correct numbers have been found a series will appear. What is the series?

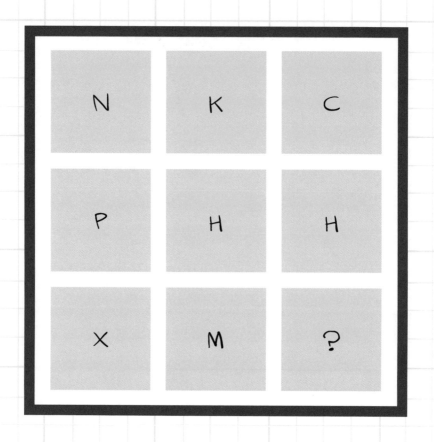

PUZZLE 75

Find a letter to complete the square in this mathematical box. Remember that letters can be used instead of numbers.

PUZZLE 76

Find a number to complete the circle.
You need to perform a very simple calculation,
but you put the result in an unexpected place.

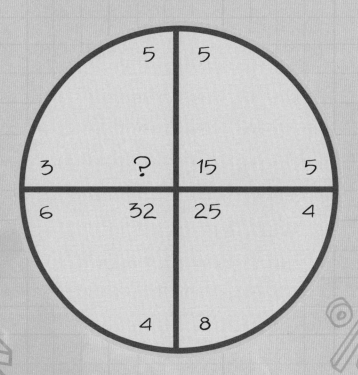

5   5

3   ?   15   5

6   32   25   4

4   8

MEGA MINDS ONLY!

PUZZLE 77

Which of the numbers in the square is
the odd one out and why?

42	15	63	6
9	81	33	21
96	16	12	48
18	60	3	90

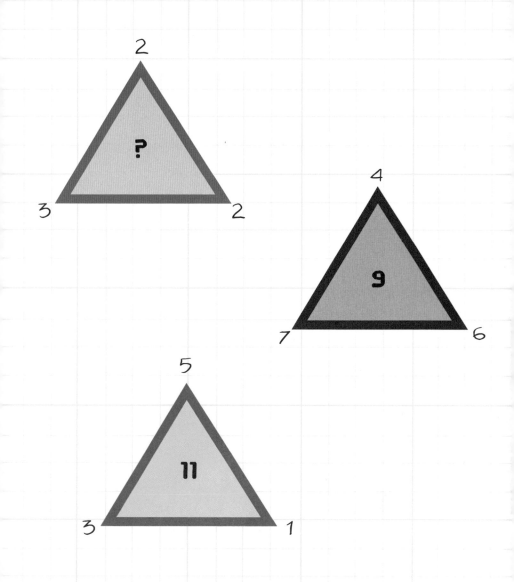

PUZZLE 78

Each number inside a triangle is the answer to a calculation involving one number from the outside of all three triangles. What number should replace the question mark?

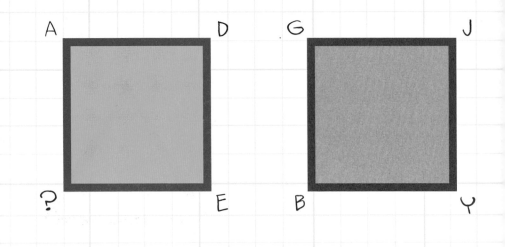

A   D   G   J

?   E   B   Y

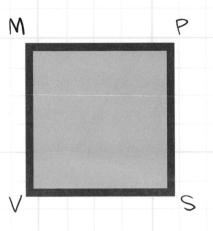

M   P

V   S

PUZZLE 79

Find the missing letter. Hint: Remember that you can write the alphabet in a circle.

PUZZLE 80

Join together the dots using only those numbers that can be divided by 5. Start at the lowest and discover the object. What is it?

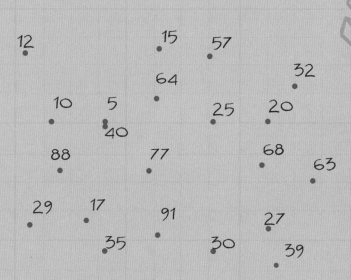

12

15   57

64   32

10   5   25   20

40

88   77   68   63

29   17   91   27   39

35   30

PUZZLE 81

Here is a series of numbers. What number should replace the question mark?

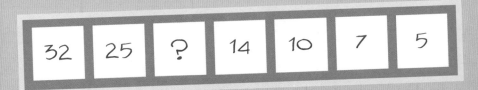

| 32 | 25 | ? | 14 | 10 | 7 | 5 |

PUZZLE 82

Using addition and subtraction of the hours, minutes and seconds, the drivers' numbers relate to the time they took to complete a race. When you have worked out the connection, you will see that there is an odd one out. Which is it?

Number 12

4:35:27

Number 11

4:26:19

Number 8

4:36:32

Number 7

4:09:07

Number 36

4:53:21

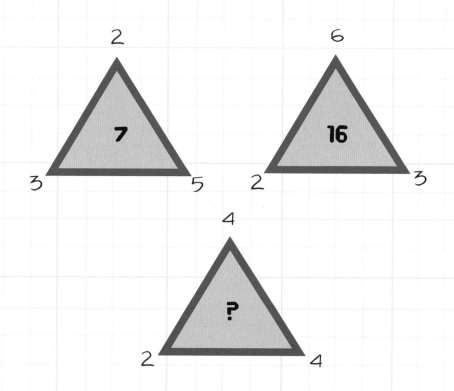

PUZZLE 83

Using multiplication and subtraction, the numbers outside each triangle relate to its central number. What number replaces the question mark?

KEEP FOCUSED!

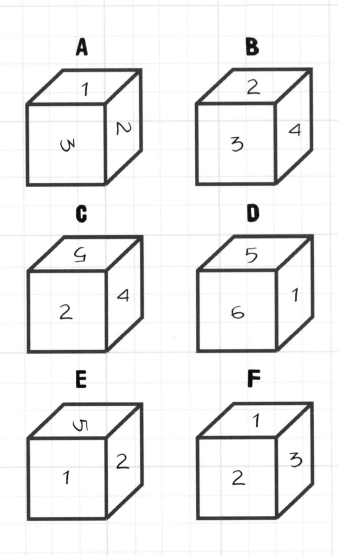

PUZZLE 84

Which of these pictures is not of the same box?

PUZZLE 85

Find the missing letter. You will find this puzzle quite easy if you imagine the letters of the alphabet going round in a circle.

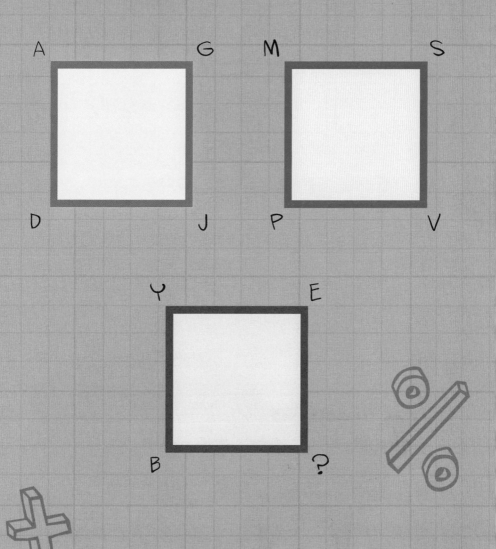

A   G   M   S

D   J   P   V

Y   E

B   ?

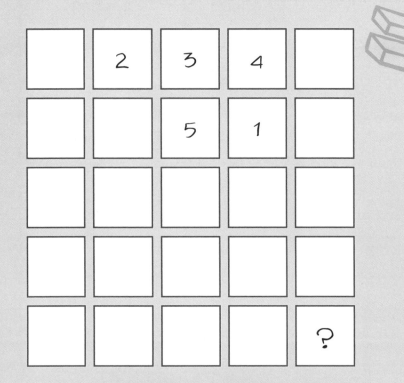

PUZZLE 86

Fill up this square with the numbers 1 to 5 so that no row, column or diagonal line of five squares uses the same number more than once. What number should replace the question mark?

GENIUSES ONLY!

PUZZLE 87

Find the missing letter to replace the question mark in the cross below.

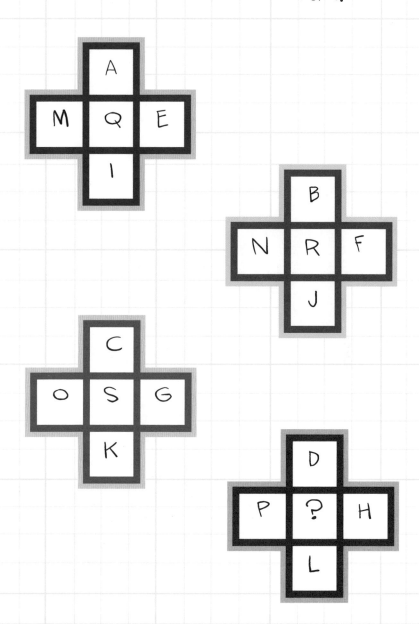

PUZZLE 88

Look at the pattern of numbers in the diagram. What number should replace the question mark?

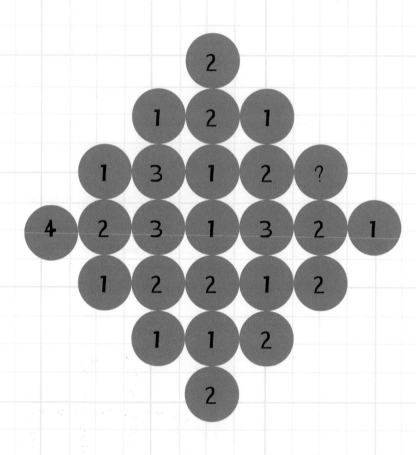

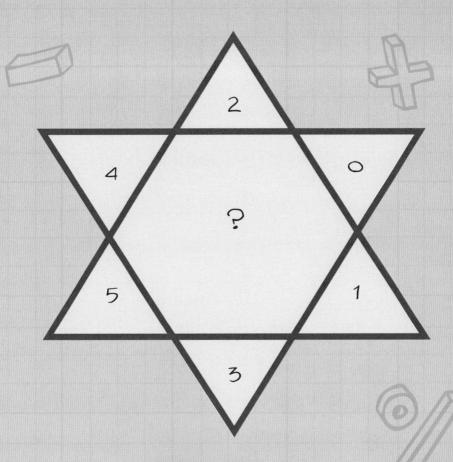

PUZZLE 89

What number will replace the
question mark in the star?

YOU'RE ONE
SMART COOKIE!

ANSWERS

ANSWER 1
50.

ANSWER 2
19. They are all prime numbers in numerical order.

ANSWER 3
A. The faces gain two elements at each step.

ANSWER 4
4.

ANSWER 5
E. The figures gain one line at each step. E should have 5 lines.

ANSWER 6
B. It is the only one wearing a hat.

ANSWER 7
7.

ANSWER 8
36. Multiply the figures diagonally across the squares and add the totals together (5 x 6 = 30) + (3 x 2 = 6) = 36.

ANSWER 9
9. The number at the end of each row is the total of the other numbers in the row.

ANSWER 10
3. Opposite sectors total the same.

ANSWER 11
28. The numbers at either side are reversed in the middle.

ANSWER 12
B. The numbers in horizontal and vertical rows are identical.

ANSWER 13
1c.

ANSWER 14
K. Going alphabetically, K is the next capital letter composed of only straight lines.

ANSWER 15
A circle. The square is twice the value of the circle and the triangle is twice the value of the square, so the triangle must be four times the circle.

ANSWER 16
9.

ANSWER 17
C. The figure turns 90° clockwise at each step. C disrupts the sequence.

ANSWER 18
15.55.09. The hours go back by 4; the minutes go forward by 4; and the seconds go back by 5.

ANSWER 19
4. It is found in 4 overlapping shapes.

ANSWER 20
C. In pattern C, the square and triangle are in the wrong order.

ANSWER 21
C. One element is added to the figure at each step.

ANSWER 22
14.

ANSWER 23
10.45.13. The hours go forward by 2, the minutes go forward by 5 and the seconds go forward by 7.

ANSWER 24
D. It is the only one which does not cut a triangle off the square.

ANSWER 25
31.

ANSWER 26
48. The numbers increase by 6 left to right along the top row and right to left along the bottom.

ANSWER 27
C. It has an odd number of elements, the others all have an even number.

ANSWER 28
23.

ANSWER 29
14. Add the three numbers at the top of each triangle and put the answer in the first triangle; then add the numbers at bottom left and put this answer in the second triangle. The three numbers on the right add up to 14.

ANSWER 30
32. Reading clockwise from the top, the first outer number in each segment increases by two each time, the second outer number increases by three and the central numbers go up by 4.

ANSWER 31
13 and one way.

ANSWER 32
G. In alphabetical order you go four places forward and then two back.

ANSWER 33
No. Amazing – but true.

ANSWER 34
1. A minus B minus C gives D.

ANSWER 35
D. The number of elements increases by two at each step, but D increases by only one.

ANSWER 36
No ways. There will always be at least one line crossing another.

ANSWER 37
30.

ANSWER 38

2. The numbers in each circle add up to 8.

ANSWER 39

15. 48 candles make 12 new ones but these 12, when burnt, will make a further 3.

ANSWER 40

27 of 2V, 5V, 10V, 20V and 50V coins.

ANSWER 41

54. All the other numbers are squares (e.g. 2 x 2 = 4, 3 x 3 = 9, 7 x 7 = 49, 9 x 9 = 81).

ANSWER 42

139. At each stage the new bottles, when broken, will make more new bottles. 279 ÷ 3 = 93. 93 ÷ 3 = 31.
31 ÷ 3 = 10 (with 1 left).
10 ÷ 3 = 3 (with 1 left).
3 ÷ 3 = 1. Take this one and add the two others left to make another 3. So, again, 3 ÷ 3 = 1. 93 + 31 + 10 + 3 + 1 + 1 = 139.

ANSWER 43

Plus, divide and multiply.

ANSWER 44

13. The two numbers at the base of each triangle are added to give the top number.

ANSWER 45

74. Double the first number, add three, double the next number, add three, etc.

ANSWER 46

131. It is the only odd number.

ANSWER 47

4.

ANSWER 48

17.

ANSWER 49

4. He makes three from the original nine, and another one from the remains of the three.

ANSWER 50

26. The sequence here is add 5, add 1, add 5, add 1, etc.

ANSWER 51

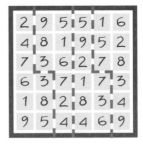

ANSWER 52

25. The sequence here is add 3, add 4, add 3, add 4.

ANSWER 53

23. All the others are multiples of 7.

ANSWER 54
16.

ANSWER 55
22. Explanation. 200 makes
20, and from the 20 he will
get another 2.

ANSWER 56
14.

ANSWER 57
55.

ANSWER 58
P. The first square misses
2 letters, the second 3. The
final square misses 4 letters at
each step.

ANSWER 59
33. Add the figure at the top
to the one on the right, then
multiply the answer by the one
on the left. Take that answer
and subtract the figure at
the bottom from it and put the
answer in the middle.

ANSWER 60
1E, 4C and 5A.

ANSWER 61
84. Reading clockwise from the
top left of each circle (left to
right) numbers increase by 7.

ANSWER 62
1. Square root ($\sqrt{}$).

ANSWER 63
17. Each letter is above or
below a number denoting its
position in the alphabet.

ANSWER 64
C. It is the only cube that has
no vowel.

ANSWER 65
7.

ANSWER 66
2.

ANSWER 67
O. The left circle contains
straight line letters, the right
has curved line letters.

ANSWER 68
13.

ANSWER 69
R. Convert the letters using
their alphabetic position. In
each column, add the top
letter to the middle to give the
one at the bottom.

ANSWER 70
Number 13. Add all the digits in
the time together to give the
car's number. It does not work
for No. 13 (it should be 11).

ANSWER 71
40.

ANSWER 72
Y. The top row added to the
central row gives the bottom
row. Y is the 25th letter.

ANSWER 73
30. Multiply all three numbers
around the triangle and put
the answer in the middle.

ANSWER 74

12, 24, 36, 48, 60, 72. The numbers increase by 12 each time.

ANSWER 75

K. In each row subtract the value of the middle letter from the left letter to get the right letter. K is the 11th letter.

ANSWER 76

24. Multiply the two outer numbers in each segment and put the answer in the middle of the next sector, reading clockwise.

ANSWER 77

16. All the other numbers are divisible by 3.

ANSWER 78

13. Add the three top numbers and put the answer in the bottom triangle; add the three right numbers and put the answer in the second triangle; and add the three left numbers and put the answer in the first triangle.

ANSWER 79

H. Reading left to right along the top, every third letter is supplied and the series continues reading right to left along the bottom.

ANSWER 80

An arrow.

ANSWER 81

19. The series of numbers decreases from the left by 7, then 6, then 5, then 4, etc.

ANSWER 82

Number 7. Add the hours and the minutes and subtract the seconds. The odd one out should be car 6 (4 + 9 (13) − 7 = 6).

ANSWER 83

14. Multiply the top and right numbers, then subtract the left number from this answer and put the new answer in the middle.

ANSWER 84

F.

ANSWER 85

H. Reading from left to right move on six letters across each row.

ANSWER 86

3.

ANSWER 87

T. Reading each cross in the order: top, right, bottom, left, middle, the sequence jumps four letters at a time.

ANSWER 88

1. The total of each horizontal line doubles from the outside to the centre.

ANSWER 89

5. All opposite points of the star add up to 5.